Medieval Castles and Knights for Kids

An Enthralling Guide to Strong Fortresses and Brave Heroes of the Middle Ages

© Copyright 2025 - All rights reserved.

The content contained within this book may not be reproduced, duplicated, or transmitted without direct written permission from the author or the publisher.

Under no circumstances will any blame or legal responsibility be held against the publisher, or author, for any damages, reparation, or monetary loss due to the information contained within this book, either directly or indirectly.

Legal Notice:

This book is copyright protected. It is only for personal use. You cannot amend, distribute, sell, use, quote, or paraphrase any part, or the content within this book, without the consent of the author or publisher.

Disclaimer Notice:

Please note the information contained within this document is for educational and entertainment purposes only. All effort has been executed to present accurate, up-to-date, reliable, and complete information. No warranties of any kind are declared or implied. Readers acknowledge that the author is not engaging in the rendering of legal, financial, medical, or professional advice. The content within this book has been derived from various sources. Please consult a licensed professional before attempting any techniques outlined in this book.

By reading this document, the reader agrees that under no circumstances is the author responsible for any losses, direct or indirect, that are incurred as a result of the use of the information contained within this document, including, but not limited to, errors, omissions, or inaccuracies.

Table of Contents

Introduction — 1

Chapter 1: Building the Medieval Castle — 2

Chapter 2: Life Inside the Castle — 11

Chapter 3: How to Become a Knight and Their Daily Life — 22

Chapter 4: Siege Warfare — 30

Chapter 5: Legendary Myths of Brave Knights — 40

Chapter 6: Legendary Medieval Castles and Their Stories — 49

Chapter 7: Incredible Medieval Faceoffs — 57

Chapter 8: Weapons and Armor: A Knight's Arsenal — 70

If you want to learn more about tons of other exciting historical periods, check out our other books! — 80

Further Reading — 81

Image Sources — 82

INTRODUCTION

The Middle Ages spanned a one-thousand-year period, starting in 476 CE following the fall of Rome and lasting until around 1450. This time was often referred to as the Dark Ages because much of Roman culture and civilization broke down, and there are fewer records of this time. However, medieval times are also known for almost feeling like a fantasy world where people lived in castles, fought dragons, and brave knights roamed the lands protecting the weak. Many modern movies, television shows, and books feature these kinds of fantasy worlds. But how many of the legends are true, and how much is fantasy?

In this book, you'll discover everything there is to know about medieval life in castles and what being a knight truly meant. You'll learn about the legendary people, battles, and castles that make this period so fascinating to us today.

So, let's travel back in time to the Middle Ages and discover what life was really like!

Chapter 1: Building the Medieval Castle

Anyone who was anyone in the Middle Ages lived in a castle, the bigger the better! Castles weren't just for living in and showing off how rich and powerful you were, though. They also had a more important purpose: They were strategically important for defense. The stronger and harder it was to attack your castle, the more power and influence you could keep.

" The word castle comes from the Latin word for fortress. "

So, let's go house hunting—medieval style!

The Evolution of Castle Design

Motte-and-Bailey

The original style of medieval castle was called a *motte-and-bailey* castle. It was introduced by the Viking settlers in France called the *Normans*.

A *motte* (rhymes with *lot*) was a mound or elevated pile of earth. These were either natural or manmade. On top of the motte was a wooden tower, and at the base was a courtyard known as a *bailey*. Inside the bailey, there were shops, houses, and stables. Surrounding the bailey was a wooden fence called a *palisade (pal-ih-sayd)*. Around the outside of the motte and the bailey was a deep ditch called a *moat* that would sometimes be filled with water. To get inside the castle, a bridge crossed the ditch into a single entrance of the motte-and-bailey.

When the Norman king, *William the Conqueror*, invaded Great Britain in 1066, he built hundreds of motte-and-bailey castles to secure his power.

However, the motte-and-bailey design was flawed, as early examples were made from wood. Although this meant they were cheap and quick to build, wood rots and is vulnerable to fire. They needed to be more durable. Later motte-and-bailey castles were made from stone.

> **FUN FACT**
> There are reportedly over 4,000 castles in England alone, and 1,000 of these were built by the Normans.

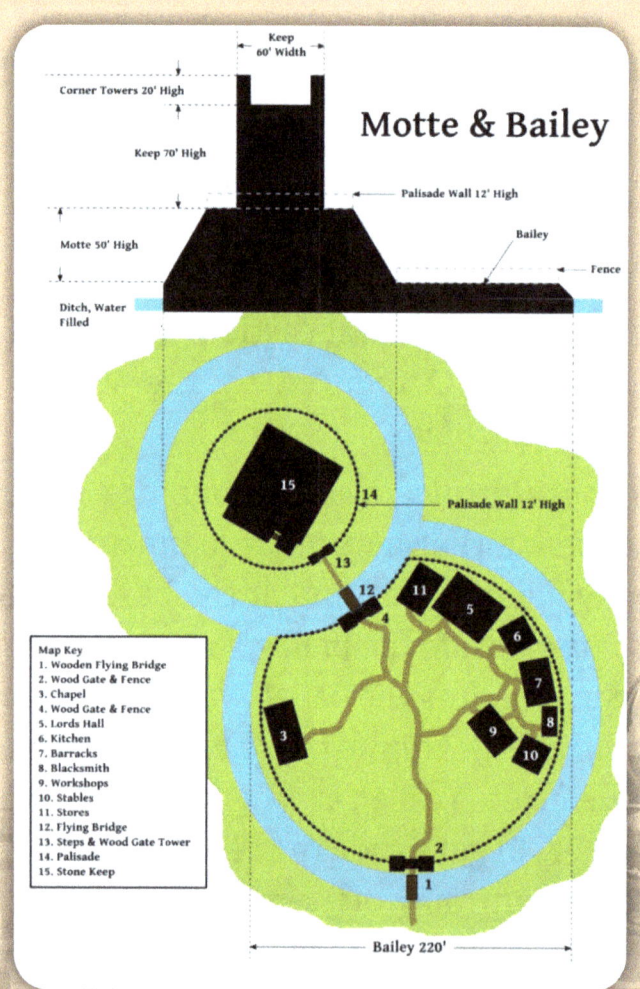

An illustration of a motte-and-bailey castle.
The keep is loosely based on Rochester and Hedingham.[1]

Stone Keep

With attacks on motte-and-bailey castles getting more advanced, castle design needed to keep up. During the eleventh century, the motte-and-bailey style was replaced with *stone keeps*. The wooden tower in the motte-and-bailey design was replaced with a stronger stone tower called a *keep*. The wooden palisades were also replaced with stone walls. These walls connected a series of defensive towers placed around the castle.

> **Fun Fact**
> William the Conqueror built the biggest castle in England, Windsor Castle, between 1070 and 1076.

> **Fun Fact**
> Perhaps one of the most famous examples of this type of keep is the White Tower at the Tower of London, which William the Conqueror began building in 1078.

Concentric Castles

The stone keep design was highly effective, but any good knight knows you can always improve your defenses! *Concentric (kun-sen-trik) castles* were similar to stone keeps but had more than one defensive outer wall. These walls were called *curtain walls*. The inner curtain walls were higher than the outer ones so guards could look out for enemies. Unlike stone keeps, not all concentric castles had a central keep.

FUN FACT

" The Tower of London can be classified as all three styles. As it developed over time, more curtain walls were added, and it changed from a motte-and-bailey stone keep castle to a concentric one. "

The Tower of London.[2]

How To Protect Your Castle

To keep your people safe, your castle needed a lot of defensive features. Here's a guide on how to make your castle the strongest in the Middle Ages!

- Build your castle up high.

    If there's a nearby mountain or hill you can use, great. If not, make one! The higher and more difficult to climb, the better.

- Dig a moat.

  Make sure to dig a deep moat around your castle. For extra protection, fill it with water so there is only one way in without having to swim or use a boat!

- Install a drawbridge.

  A regular bridge leaves your castle vulnerable. Install a *drawbridge* that can be lifted up to make your moat complete. It's easy to put it down when you need to go out or let friends in.

- Add a portcullis.

  If someone manages to cross your drawbridge, fortify your entrance with a *portcullis (port-kull-iss)*. This heavy metal gate can be lowered to trap intruders in the gatehouse or keep them out entirely. Plus, the metal spikes at the bottom might catch someone too slow!

Fun Fact

> In the entrance tunnels, defending soldiers would pour hot oil or boiling water onto invading men through holes in the ceiling. Ouch!

- Build tall circular towers.

  Forget the original square design. Rounded towers are far stronger! Make sure you have plenty of tall towers around your curtain wall to look out for enemies.

FUN FACT

> Square castles were also more vulnerable, as enemies could dig under the corners and make them collapse!

- Add battlements to your castle roof.

    Battlements are walls that stand up on your roof. The *merlons (mer-luns)* (high walls) are perfect to hide behind while the *crenels (kren-uls)* (lower gaps) allow you to fire arrows.

A drawing of someone firing an arrow out of the crenels of a castle's battlements.[3]

- Install plenty of arrow slits.

    You need more than just crenels to fire at your enemies. Across your castle, add lots of small, thin windows that are perfect for firing out of but not big enough for enemies to fire into them.

- Install secret passageways.

    You might find that your enemy attacks your castle for a long period. While they can't get in, you can't get out! This means you may run low on food or water. Install some secret hidden passageways that can be used to escape, access a water source, hide valuables, or launch a surprise attack if the enemy gets inside!

- Include a dungeon.

    Just in case someone manages to get inside or you have any prisoners you need to keep locked away, be sure to include a dungeon in the basement of your castle!

Fun Fact

> Dungeons were originally built for protection. During an enemy attack, people would hide here. Attacks could last so long that people ran out of food and would eat rats or leather shoes!

The Great Hall

No castle is complete without a great hall. This is the centerpiece of your castle where all your social and *administrative* activities (like planning, organizing, and keeping track of stuff) will take place. (The great hall started as a place for people to sleep and eat, but it evolved into much more. It held great banquets and courts where the common folk could get an audience with the lord of the castle.)

Your great hall needs to be large and beautifully decorated to show how rich and important you are. It also needs to be located somewhere safe, either on a low floor within the keep or in a building within the castle's bailey. The key features all medieval great halls must have are a rectangular shape, a high and beautifully decorated ceiling, plenty of big windows, a stage where you can sit above your subjects, and a large central fireplace. Be sure to include your coat of arms all around the hall so people know who's boss!

Chapter 1 Activity

Design your own medieval castle! You can either draw a picture of it or create a 3D model using cardboard by following this YouTube tutorial.

https://youtu.be/HGH2bteGpTA?si=W4ZC6NU7FziJR4jz

Chapter 2: Life Inside the Castle

Daily life inside the castle would be very different depending on your social status. Medieval Britain operated under a *feudal (fyoo-duhl)* system. Under the feudal system, the king and nobles who owned land were at the top of society, and soldiers and peasants were underneath them. In exchange for fighting or farming the land, the lower classes were given protection and a place to live. At the center of the land was the castle.

The King of the Castle

The most important person in the castle was the owner. This could be a king, lord, lady, noble, or knight. The more wealthy and powerful a person was, the more land and castles they had.

> **Fun Fact**
> Some kings in places like England had so many castles that there were some they had never visited!

This meant some people did not live in just one castle but would travel between several castles. When they visited their castles, they would often arrive with hundreds of people, so it was no simple task to host them all!

The owner of the castle had private living quarters in the safest part of the castle where only certain people could go. The quarters could be as simple as a bedroom, bathroom, a space to entertain guests, and sometimes a chapel. Some were grander and located in a separate building—a castle within the castle that protected you even if the main one was captured.

Life for the castle's most important people was pretty comfortable in comparison to life for the rest of the inhabitants, though not as comfy as our homes today!

Medieval private bedroom.[4]

A Typical Day Living in Your Medieval Castle

Breakfast

What your day would look like in your journey back to the Middle Ages depends on what job you had. If you were a servant, you would need to wake up before everyone else when it's still dark to light the fires in the great hall and the kitchen, bake bread, and prepare breakfast. If you were lucky enough to be more important than a servant, but not a noble, you'd be awakened at sunrise by the sound of a trumpet to eat the simple breakfast the servants prepared. If you were at the top of society, you could lie in bed until ten or even midday if you wished! But a chunk of that time might be spent having your maids help you get dressed into your medieval clothing.

In medieval times, it was pretty normal for peasants to only eat two meals a day: breakfast and dinner in the mid-afternoon. The rich would have three, with two smaller meals on either side of their big main meal. Daily breakfast was fairly simple, usually just some bread or porridge. If you were more important, you might get some cheese, meat, or meat drippings to go with it. You would wash your breakfast down with a glass of water or ale—a type of beer.

Fun Fact

> It's a myth that people in medieval times didn't drink water. However, they were aware that unclean water could make you sick, so they drank beer or wine instead if no clean water was available.

Medieval bakers.[5]

Daily Tasks

Once you'd filled your belly, you would get to work. Servants cleaned and took care of the castle, cooks prepared more food for dinner, grooms took care of the horses, and so on. Tradespeople such as blacksmiths made horseshoes, weapons, and other metal items; carpenters worked with wood; and masons worked with stone to make repairs to the castle.

> **Fun Fact**
>
> Not all servants were poor. Children of wealthy families would be sent to work as pages and damsels, learning how to fit in with high society and caring for the lords and ladies.

Knights and their squires would spend most of the day practicing and honing their skills or teaching others—and, of course, protecting the castle from enemy attacks. Priests would offer spiritual guidance and hold sermons.

The men of the upper classes would have lots of meetings about running the castle, finances, trading, legal matters, warfare, and other such things. They would also have some leisure time to hunt or practice sword fighting or other hobbies. The noble ladies of the castle would pursue their own hobbies, such as sewing or playing instruments. The lady of the castle may also meet with other women to help them with women's issues or instruct the servants about running the household.

Children would be given lessons on religion and things important to their future life. Poorer children would be more likely to learn from family members, while noble ones would have teachers responsible for their lessons.

A medieval classroom.[6]

Feast Time!

The cooks in the castle would be especially busy, as they needed to feed hundreds of people every day. On feast days, it was even busier, as they would have to cook a variety of extravagant dishes to impress their guests. Dinner would be served in the great hall. And, although it wasn't always a grand affair, the medieval lords and ladies loved to throw feasts!

Where you would sit depended on your social status. The lord of the castle would sit on a raised platform at the top table in the hall with his most important and influential friends. The farther toward the back of the hall you sat, the less important you were. This was because the best dishes would be served to the most important people first. By the time food reached the back, all the good stuff would have been gobbled down!

A Rich Banquet: c. 1460
The walls are hung with tapestry representing a battle scene; over the master of the house is a canopy and behind him a wicker fire-screen. The carver has a towel over his shoulder; above him is the steward with his rod of office

A rich banquet.[7]

The wealthiest people in medieval society would get to eat more meat. In addition to fresh meat, it could be salted or smoked to preserve it. Dishes included meats similar to what we eat today: pork, beef, mutton, and poultry such as chicken, duck, geese, pheasant, or even pigeon. But they also ate even more unusual birds like cranes or herons. The more adventurous would even serve swans or peacocks!

Animals that had been killed during a hunt would be served up. They could be as small as rabbits and hares or as impressive as a deer or wild boar. Depending on how close you lived to the ocean, fish would also be a regular mealtime dish. All this meat was served in many ways, from boiling and grilling to meatballs or pies.

> **Fun Fact**
> "Medieval nobles ate whale meat. It was the most expensive and exotic dish, nicknamed the "royal fish.""

All of this meat would be accompanied by a selection of in-season vegetables that were available on the land. Bread and other grains would also be included. There was even dessert! This would include cheese and fruits.

Wine and ale were the drinks of choice, and there would be plenty to make people merry. Wine was considered a more distinguished drink for the upper classes at feasts. Even the children would drink beer and wine!

> **Fun Fact**
> "This might sound like a lot of food because it is! Up to ten courses could be served, and it was seen as a virtue to eat a lot."

Entertainment

Of course, no royal feast would be complete without some entertainment. Throughout the feast, minstrels would play music on lutes (a type of stringed instrument a bit like a guitar) and sing, or someone might play the harp. Jesters, acrobats, and jugglers would also perform. Jesters were meant to make people laugh and were also called fools. They were often mocked but could get away with making fun of powerful people if they were clever about it.

Fun Fact

> One jester was sentenced to death when he offended a king with his jokes. When told he could choose how he wished to die for his execution, he replied "of old age" and was pardoned because of his wit!

After the meal, there would be dancing, and some guests might perform songs of their own. People would also play games such as chess, backgammon, or dice and bet on them.

A medieval feast and a jester (in green, yellow, and red). The Lancelot romance, France, fifteenth century.[8]

Bedtime

At the end of the day, the lord of the manor and his people would retire to their private quarters, leaving the servants to clean up after everybody. Some castles had special barracks for the knights to sleep in. Everyone else had to find a spot to sleep in the great hall. This meant you could get stuck sleeping on the hard floor or in another equally uncomfortable room if you weren't lucky!

You wouldn't even get any privacy to use the toilet, as all the bathrooms in the main castle were communal. But you'd at least be happy you weren't a *gong farmer*! This was the job of some poor souls.

Toilets were called gongs (as were number twos). Since there weren't flushing toilets, you would poo sitting on a wooden or stone bench with holes in it, which would hang out over the edge of the castle wall. Your poop would land in the moat, a pit, or on the ground outside.

When the smell got too bad, it was the gong farmers' job to collect all the waste and take it away—usually to be used as fertilizer. Of course, the job was a disgusting and smelly one that people didn't want to do, so it was at least quite well paid.

Fun Fact

"The job of a gong farmer could be quite dangerous. In 1325, one poor soul fell into a cesspit and drowned—what a way to go!"

A photo of medieval toilets from the outside of Portchester Castle, England.⁹

Chapter 2 Activity

Imagine you are living in a medieval castle. Decide on any job and position in society you would like and write a story or journal entry about your life. Get as creative as you like, but try to think of what your life might have been like!

Perhaps even write about being a noble and then also about being a servant and imagine how different life was for them.

Chapter 3: How to Become a Knight and Their Daily Life

Knights played an important role in medieval society. Today, people are granted knighthoods for good deeds, but in the Middle Ages, knights were the most skilled and accomplished soldiers. They mostly fought on horseback and would train for years to become knights. Being a knight was expensive. You must be able to buy weapons, a horse, and chainmail armor, and you needed to be taught. For this reason, knights were generally the sons of wealthy and important men.

A drawing of a knight on horseback.[10]

So, what would your life be like if you wanted to become a knight during the Middle Ages?

As young as seven years old, you would be sent to live in the household of a lord to become a page and start your knighthood training. First, you would have to learn to read, write, and hunt. You would also be expected to do chores to earn your keep. Pages would also help older knights by looking after their horses, cleaning their armor and weapons, and packing the bags when going on long trips into battle with them.

Around age twelve to fifteen, you would become a squire. As a squire, you would work directly with a knight who would teach you to use swords and spears. You would also start practicing moving around in the heavy armor that knights wore—a difficult task! But, as a squire, you could buy your very own armor instead of borrowing it. As a squire, you needed to learn the seven agilities: horse riding, shooting, swimming, climbing, wrestling, fencing, and long jumping. You also needed to learn how to dance!

By twenty-one, you would finally be eligible to get your knighthood. The men with the most military experience and success would be more desirable. You could get your knighthood earlier if you did a particularly brave or impressive thing, such as protecting a royal person in a battle.

Becoming a knight was a big deal, and there was a grand ceremony to mark the occasion. This would usually be held around an important holiday such as Easter or Christmas or during an important wedding. On the night before, you would have to take a ritual bath and say special prayers. During the ceremony, you would swear an oath of *fealty (fee-uhl-tee)*, promising that you would remain loyal to the lord knighting you. The master of ceremony would *dub* you by lightly touching a sword on each of your shoulders.

A knight being dubbed. Accolade by Edmund Blair Leighton."

As a knight, you would be required to fight for your lord. In return, your lord would bestow you with land, money, and even titles and power if you were successful in battle.

FUN FACT

"The monarch of England still dubs people receiving knighthoods today."

As a knight, you would be expected to live by a *code of chivalry (shi-vuhl-ree)*. In addition to being brave and skilled in battle, you had to defend the weak and the poor, respect women, and be generous and courteous. (Being courteous means being polite and showing kindness and respect to others.)

Knights were expected to be courteous even when fighting an enemy. It was not courteous to injure another man's horse. You couldn't fight an enemy who had fallen from his horse until he had remounted or you had gotten off yours. If you beat your enemy and he asked to be taken prisoner and shown mercy, it was not courteous to kill him.

Knights would take part in tournaments to show off their skills, courage, and strength as a knight. In these tournaments, knights would compete in different challenges, such as sword fighting or *jousting (jau-stuhng)*. Jousting was when two competitors would ride toward each other on horseback carrying *lances* (a type of spear) made from wood. The goal was to try to knock your opponent off his horse. Points were also given for striking your opponent, hitting the crest of his helmet, or surviving the most undefeated jousts. Tournaments were also a good way to practice your skills between battles.

> **FUN FACT**
> "Hitting your opponent's horse instantly got you disqualified."

When tournaments originally started in France, they were incredibly dangerous and more like miniature battles. There were no rules, and several knights could gang up on another knight, taking his valuable possessions when he lost. In one tournament alone, sixty men died! The church condemned the tournaments, and England outlawed them for a while.

Changes were made to make tournaments safer for participants (although they weren't without risk) and allow people to watch them. People loved to watch tournaments, and they were a very popular source of entertainment. Knights would fight for the honor of a chosen lady, who might present them with a token of her affection and support. Success in tournaments could make knights rich and famous. Sir John Cornwall was so good at jousting that he was married to a princess as a prize!

> **Fun Fact**
> King Henry VIII of England was a renowned jouster in his youth and loved to host tournaments.

A drawing of two men jousting.[12]

If you were a knight between 1095 and 1291, it's very likely you would have been part of the *crusades*. This was a series of wars between the European Christians and the Muslims over the control of the Holy Land, including Jerusalem.

During the crusades, there was a famous Christian order of knights called the *Knights Templar*. Their main role was to protect Christians making a pilgrimage to the Holy Land and fighting in the wars. They wore white tunics with red crosses over their armor to show their order.

> **FUN FACT**
> "The word "crusade" comes from the Latin word crux, which means cross."

Chapter 3 Activity

Can you figure out which statements are true and which are false?

1. True or False: A young man became a knight by first becoming a page and then a squire before finally being knighted.

2. True or False: Knights would be dubbed with a sword during their knighthood ceremony.

3. True or False: The purpose of tournaments was solely for the entertainment of the local population.

4. True or False: Anyone could be a knight, and it didn't cost a lot of money to become one.

5. True or False: Knights lived by a code of chivalry that required them to be respectful, courteous, and generous.

6. True or False: Tournaments were very safe because they did not use real weapons.

7. True or False: The Knights Templar were Muslim soldiers during the crusades.

Chapter 3 Answers

1. True or False: A young man became a knight by first becoming a page and then a squire before finally being knighted. **True.**

2. True or False: Knights would be dubbed with a sword during their knighthood ceremony. **True.**

3. True or False: The purpose of tournaments was solely for the entertainment of the local population. **False. It was also a way for knights to practice their skills.**

4. True or False: Anyone could be a knight, and it didn't cost a lot of money to become one. **False. Mostly only the wealthy became knights, as it was very expensive.**

5. True or False: Knights lived by a code of chivalry that required them to be respectful, courteous, and generous. **True.**

6. True or False: Tournaments were very safe because they did not use real weapons. **False. Tournaments could still result in injury or death.**

7. True or False: The Knights Templar were Muslim soldiers during the crusades. **False. The Knights Templar fought for the Christians during the crusades.**

Chapter 4: Siege Warfare

A *siege (seej)* is when an enemy army surrounds a city, castle, or fortress and cuts off their supplies in the hope that they'll surrender. This is often used when an army cannot easily or quickly *breach* (break through) the defenses of the place they're trying to attack and the enemy won't surrender. By the Middle Ages, sieges had been used as a military tactic for thousands of years, with the earliest known example taking place around 3000 BCE in ancient Egypt.

A drawing showing the many siege tactics used in the Middle Ages.[13]

Because castles were so popular and difficult to breach, siege warfare became a hugely important part of warfare in medieval Europe. It became more common than traditional battles. Winning a siege could mean you won the war! As castles became stronger and harder to attack, sieges became harder, and soldiers had to think of new ways to force the enemy to surrender.

Imagine that, as a medieval noble, you have an enemy castle you want to attack. With all the ingenious defenses medieval castles have, it seems almost impossible to win. So, you have to be very creative with your siege.

The simplest method of *besieging* a castle is to completely surround the fortress to try to cut off any supplies, including food, water, or reinforcements. Then, you simply have to wait. Once the people inside begin to starve or run out of water, they will be forced to surrender or avoid death.

To ensure that no food supplies could somehow slip into the castle, it might be a good idea to burn all the surrounding farmland and villages so there's nothing for your enemy to smuggle in.

Although this siege method works, it's a very slow method. Castles were usually well prepared for attacks, with plenty of food and drinks, so it could take months. Your soldiers could also suffer from food and water shortages while waiting for the enemy to surrender.

Plus, if the castle you're attacking is on the coast, it could receive supplies on boats from the sea. So, you also need a naval force to stop this from happening. Even if the castle isn't on the coast, there could be secret tunnels that allow people to sneak out without your knowledge. Or, if the city is very big, you may not be able to completely encircle it to make sure no one gets out.

Photo of the ruins of Dunluce Castle, Ireland.[14]

So, what other options do you have?

Well, one option is to build a siege castle of your own right outside the castle you're besieging. Yes, that's right—people really did that! By building your own castle outside the enemy's castle gate, your forces can leave to fight elsewhere while you're in a siege-off!

You should hope that the siege ends as quickly as possible because the longer the siege takes, the more expensive it gets. Many of your soldiers may not be willing to stay for that long or may succumb to sickness. The bigger or better known your army is, the more likely the siege will be short and your enemy will surrender quicker.

> **Fun Fact**
>
> King Henry I (1100-1135 CE) and Joan of Arc (1412-1431 CE) were two famous examples of this. When they turned up to a siege in person, their reputations made the enemy surrender faster.

If your siege is dragging on too long, you might want to consider sending in a messenger to discuss the terms of a surrender. For example, you could offer to allow the innocent people inside to safely leave. If they still refuse, you might need to use some scare tactics. Catapulting the heads of captured and killed enemies is a sure way to ruffle some feathers! If you can find someone close to the leaders inside the castle, you could also threaten to kill them unless the enemy surrenders.

If those tactics are a bit too brutal for you, then a *battering ram* is also a good option to try. A battering ram is a big, heavy

> **Fun Fact**
>
> The longest siege in medieval England was on Kenilworth Castle in 1266. It lasted 172 days—almost six months!

beam of wood with a sharp metal end used to ram against castles. The goal is to break a hole in the castle so you can get inside. Originally, these were made from wood and had a ram's head carved at the end. Battering rams can be carried by a group of men or on a device with wheels. By suspending it from a frame, you can also swing your battering ram with more force.

You might think the most obvious target is the entrance, as the door seems like the weakest point. However, as castle gates grew stronger, the door actually became one of the strongest points. So, it could also be a good idea to try ramming a weaker wall.

Medieval battering ram, Mercato San Severino, Italy, town hall.[15]

While you're trying to breach the walls with your battering ram, you might also consider trying to launch missiles over the walls using catapults and artillery. Heavy boulders or flaming objects are popular and effective missiles. These would start fires within the castle's stone walls, where there are wooden structures.

If you were leading a siege after 1326 CE, there may have been the option of gunpowder cannons called *bombards*. However, the early designs usually killed the person who fired them, so they weren't ideal! By the fifteenth century, cannons had been perfected. They were so effective that they eventually led to the end of siege warfare.

A siege tower.[16]

Another way to go over the top of a castle is to build a *siege tower*. This is made from wood and can be wheeled up to a wall. You need to make your siege tower higher than the walls of the castle so your archers can fire down against defensive attacks. Once you've cleared the way, you can try to climb over the walls.

If going over the walls of the castle you're attacking doesn't work, you could try going under. By digging tunnels, you could either gain access inside or cause the foundation of the walls to collapse. Of course, if the castle was built on solid rock, this isn't possible. This tactic also comes with risks, as the defenders could launch a counterattack and collapse your tunnel on top of you!

If all of that fails, try the sneaky route! Sending fake letters from the castle's leader ordering surrender is one option, or you could send men inside in disguise. If you have a prominent knight that the citizens believes is on their side, he could trick them and talk his way in. Spies are also a great way to learn as much about your enemy's weaknesses as possible. Finally, you could try dirty tactics—quite literally—such as polluting the water supply or launching over manure or dead animals to try to spread disease.

Once you've finally defeated your enemy, if they didn't surrender quickly, it's unlikely you will be very nice to them.

Stealing all the loot and killing the people inside was a common occurrence. Religious people and churches were left unharmed out of respect, and soldiers were sometimes treated more leniently than others involved in the fighting since they were simply doing their jobs.

If the castle was a particularly strong one in a strategic position, you might want to restore it so you can use it. If not, destroy it. This will send a message and prevent any enemies from taking control of it and restoring it for themselves.

Fun Fact

" Carlisle Castle was the main point of defense for the English against attacks from the Scots for more than 500 years and the most besieged castle in Britain. It was besieged a whopping ten times! "

Chapter 4 Activity

Can you fill in the crossword below based on the following clues?

1. Something you use to knock down a door or wall that can be suspended and swung for more force.
2. The type of warfare we learned about in this chapter.
3. A weapon used to launch items over walls or long distances.
4. A tall wooden structure that would be built higher than the walls, wheeled up close to them, and used to climb over.
5. The type of people/organizations who were spared once a castle had been conquered.
6. The name for the earliest form of gunpowder cannon.

Chapter 4 Answers

				4								
				S							6	
				I			5				B	
				E			R				O	
		3		G			E				M	
		B		E			L				B	
1	B	A	T	T	E	R	I	N	G	R	A	M
		T		O			G				R	
		A		W			I				D	
		P		E			O				S	
		U		R			U					
		L				2	S	I	E	G	E	
		T										

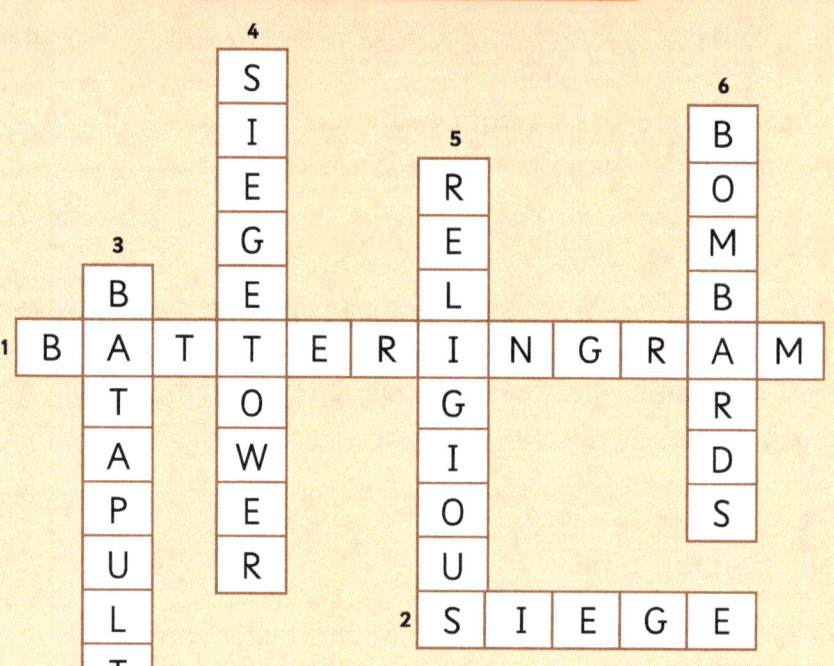

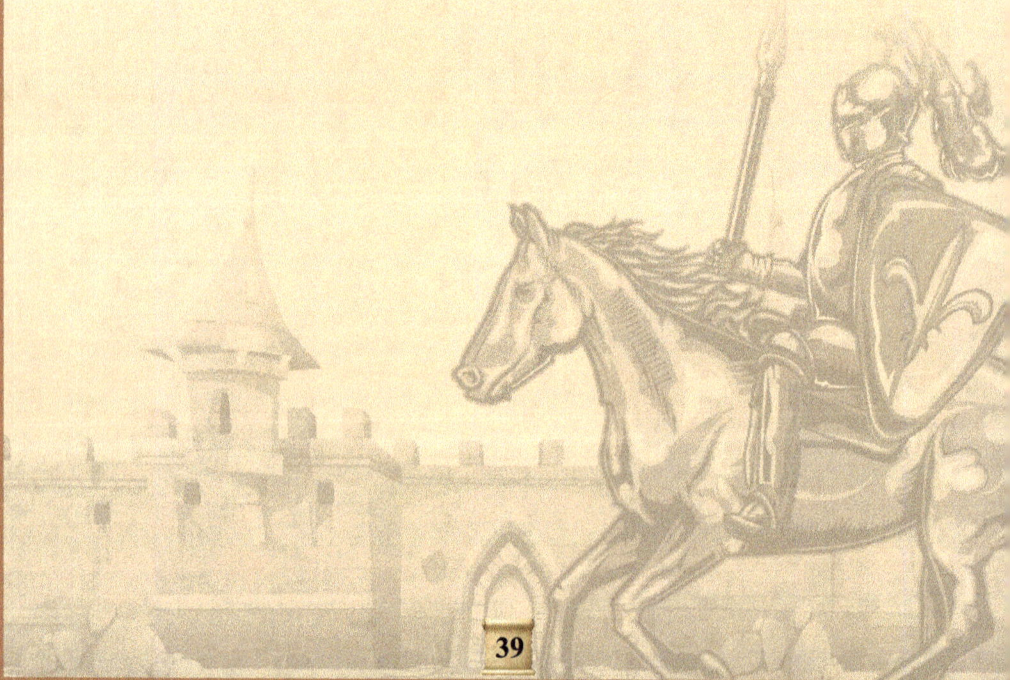

Chapter 5: Legendary Myths of Brave Knights

It isn't just today that we're fascinated by knights and their adventures. During the Middle Ages, people were just as interested in tales of brave knights and heroes as we are. These legends were passed down through word of mouth, and many were eventually written down in books. Many of them are made up, but they demonstrate the chivalric values that medieval people admired. We refer to this as medieval folklore. In addition to covering stories of knights, folklore also talks about animals, religion, magic, and more.

Fun Fact

> Many of the fairy tales you know today started as medieval folklore and changed over time. These tales are most famously known today from the Grimm brothers' book of fairy tales and later Disney movie versions.

The Legend of King Arthur

Perhaps the most famous legendary knight and story is of King Arthur. The stories that feature him are known as the *Arthurian legend*. These tales blend myth and history. Some historians believe Arthur was a real person who may have led battles for the Celts against the invading Saxons around 400–500 CE. Rumors of his heroism may have been passed down and elaborated over the years to form the stories we know now.

According to the stories, *King Uther Pendragon (yoo-thuh pendra-gn)* gave his young son Arthur to a wizard named

Merlin. In one tale, Merlin magically placed a sword named *Excalibur (ex-cah-luh-ber)* in stone. Whoever could pull the sword from the stone was Uther's true heir and would become king. The strongest men in the kingdom all tried, but no one could make it move even an inch. Then, a young, scrawny Arthur decided to give it a go. Everyone laughed, but the sword easily came away in his hands. He was declared the true heir, and the sword remained his throughout his rule.

Arthur pulling the sword from the stone.[17]

> **FUN FACT**
> - In another legend, a mysterious magical fairy called the Lady of the Lake gives Excalibur to Arthur.
> - The 1963 Disney movie The Sword in the Stone tells the story of a young Arthur and his adventures with Merlin.

The Knights of the Round Table

King Arthur had a group of the best and most trusted knights in his kingdom working for him. They lived with him and his wife *Queen Guinevere (gwi-nuh-veeuh)* in his castle, *Camelot (cam-uh-lot)*. When King Arthur and his knights were discussing important matters, he decided they would sit at a round table instead of a rectangular one. This way, they were all equal. No one was seated nearer the top or bottom of the table.

Although Arthur treated them as equals, some of the Knights of the Round Table are more famous than others. *Sir Lancelot (laan-suh-lot)* is perhaps the most well-known. He was reportedly the son of a king and raised by fairies. He was the strongest, noblest, and most skilled of all the knights. Sadly, Lancelot fell in love with Arthur's wife, Guinevere. The love triangle caused Arthur to lash out against them and sentence his wife to death. This led to the downfall of Camelot as Lancelot rose up to save her.

Sir Galahad (gah-luh-had), the son of Lancelot, appears later in the Arthurian legends and is well-known for being the purest of Arthur's knights. In many Arthurian stories, the

Knights of the Round Table search for the Holy Grail. It is Sir Galahad who finally succeeds in finding it.

King Arthur's Round Table, engraved from a fourteenth-century miniature.[18]

The Canterbury Tales

The Canterbury Tales, written by the fourteenth-century poet *Geoffrey Chaucer*, features a group of thirty *pilgrims* (people who journey to an important religious site) traveling from London to Canterbury to visit the tomb of *Saint Thomas Becket* (a former archbishop of Canterbury) at Canterbury Cathedral. The shrine became famous for supposedly granting miracles. In the Middle Ages, it was one of the four most popular places to go on a *pilgrimage*.

On the way, the characters tell stories, and these make up *The Canterbury Tales*. The stories became so popular during the Middle Ages that Chaucer was invited to read them to the king and his court!

> **FUN FACT**
> The Canterbury Tales was one of the first books written in English. Chaucer is considered the "father of English literature."

There are twenty-three complete tales and one half-finished tale in the collection. Some of the stories are serious and religious, and some are funny or even rude! King Arthur even shows up in one of the most famous stories, *The Wife of Bath's Tale*.

The Canterbury Pilgrims Copper engraving printed on paper.[19]

The Wife of Bath's Tale

In this tale, a man sentenced to death is told by Queen Guinevere that he will be spared if he can find out within a year what women want most in the world. He sets off on his mission, but everyone the man asks has a different answer, and he starts getting desperate. Time is running out.

Then, he meets an old *crone* (a magical, ugly old woman in folklore). She tells him she will give him the right answer if he pledges himself to her. Without another choice, he agrees. When the man returns to court, he says that what women want most is to be in charge of men. All the women agree, and his life is spared.

However, the man is then horrified to find that the crone wants him to marry her. He begs not to but is forced to because of his pledge. After the wedding, the crone gives him a choice. She can be ugly but loyal and good, or beautiful and young but not nice and unfaithful. He thinks about it and answers that he trusts her to choose whatever she thinks is best. Because he gives her what women most want—power over her own decisions—she becomes beautiful, loyal, and good, and they live happily ever after.

The man and the crone, The Wife of Bath's Tale.[20]

Saint George and the Dragon

People believed dragons were real in medieval times. Dragons were tied into Christian stories to teach people moral lessons. They represented evil and the devil and were usually slain by a knight or other hero in the tales.

Perhaps the most famous tale is of *Saint George* slaying a dragon. This story became popular in the twelfth century and has some truth to it: George really existed. Saint George was a knight in the Third Crusade. Legend has it that while in Libya, he came across a ferocious dragon who had been eating all the town's sheep. But once the sheep were gone, he began demanding that the town sacrifice young maidens. Soon, only one maiden was left, the Princess of England. The king promised that whoever slayed the dragon could marry his daughter. George bravely approached the dragon's lair and struck it with his spear. But it couldn't pierce the dragon's scales, and the spear shattered into pieces. Unafraid, George fought the dragon with his sword and successfully killed it, saving the princess.

> **FUN FACT**
> Saint George is the patron saint of England. However, it's believed that Saint George wasn't English but was, in fact, from Turkey!

Chapter 5 Activity

Fill in the blanks below!

Stories that feature the famous King Arthur are part of the _____ legend. Arthur was the son of King _____ Pendragon and was raised by the wizard _____. In one story, he pulled his sword, _____, from a magical stone when no one else could.

Arthur lived in _____ Castle with his wife Queen _____. He had an order of knights who would sit at a _____ _____.

One of Arthur's knights, Sir _____, fell in love with the queen. This knight's son was called Sir _____ and famously found the Holy ____.

_____ _____ wrote The _____ Tales. The collection of tales is about thirty _____ traveling from London to visit the tomb of Saint _____ _____ at Canterbury Cathedral.

Chapter 5 Answers

Stories that feature the famous King Arthur are part of the **Arthurian** legend. Arthur was the son of King **Uther** Pendragon and was raised by the wizard **Merlin**. In one story, he pulled his sword, **Excalibur**, from a magical stone when no one else could.

Arthur lived in **Camelot** Castle with his wife Queen **Guinevere**. He had an order of knights who would sit at a **round table**.

One of Arthur's knights, Sir **Lancelot**, fell in love with the queen. This knight's son was called Sir **Galahad** and famously found the Holy **Grail**.

Geoffrey Chaucer wrote The Canterbury Tales. The collection of tales is about thirty **pilgrims** traveling from London to visit the tomb of Saint **Thomas Becket** at Canterbury Cathedral.

Chapter 6: Legendary Medieval Castles and Their Stories

Hundreds of medieval castles are still standing today. Most are in Europe, but some are farther away. In this chapter, we'll talk about some of the most famous and legendary castles.

Windsor Castle

We're confident you've heard of this castle! Windsor Castle is home to the British royal family and is the largest inhabited castle in the world. Located in the town of Windsor in Berkshire, England, the castle complex takes up around thirteen thousand acres of land. The castle complex was added to over hundreds of years, starting in 1070 CE.

The castle started as a humble defensive motte-and-bailey castle, but later kings added to it and began living there, partly thanks to the nearby woodlands that were popular for hunting. It soon became one of the most expensive secular (non-religious) building projects in medieval England.

An image from a set of eight extra-illustrated volumes of A tour in Wales by Thomas Pennant (1726-1798) that chronicle the three journeys he made through Wales between 1773 and 1776.[21]

> ## Fun Fact
>
> In 1992, a huge fire in Windsor Castles damaged over 100 rooms! 1.5 million gallons of water were needed to put out the fire that raged for fifteen hours. It took five years and cost £37 million to restore it.

Bran Castle

Also known as Dracula's Castle, it is believed that this Transylvanian fortress inspired the writings of Bram Stoker, who wrote the novel *Dracula* about a vampire of the same name. This spooky castle helped make the vampire genre so popular today! As with many medieval castles, it was built with wood in 1212 before being destroyed by enemies and rebuilt from stone. As the legendary home of Count Dracula, the castle is now a museum.

Bran Castle.[22]

> **FUN FACT**
>
> " There was a real-life brutal ruler who lived in this castle and inspired Dracula: Vlad III, better known as Vlad the Impaler. He placed his victims on spikes and stakes as punishment. "

Tintagel Castle

Tintagel Castle in Cornwall, England, is not particularly impressive. What makes it interesting is the story behind it. In 1233, Richard Earl of Cornwall, younger brother of King Henry III, made a strange and seemingly poor deal. He exchanged three manors for this small, *inhospitable* (unwelcome), rocky land. The reason? Tintagel was featured in two legends about kings that were popular among medieval lords.

Tintagel Castle ruins.[23]

According to one legend in *History of the Kings of Britain* by the cleric Geoffrey of Monmouth, mythological king Uther Pendragon falls in love with a married woman. The woman's husband hides her away in an impenetrable castle, Tintagel. Uther realizes he cannot get inside using ordinary means, so the wizard Merlin gives him a potion that makes him look like the woman's husband, and he easily walks inside the castle.

Tintagel Castle was also in another story that became part of the legends surrounding King Arthur.

Malbork Castle

Located in Malbork, Poland, this castle is the largest in the world by surface area. It was built in 1274 by a Roman Catholic order of German knights called the *Teutonic Knights*. This impressive castle is actually made up of three castles, hundreds of buildings, and two defensive ring walls.

The Teutonic Knights formed during the crusades. Despite changing, being defeated, and being pushed out of areas for hundreds of years, the Teutonic Order still exists today—but as a charitable group, not a military one.

Fun Fact

" Malbork Castle (as well as many medieval castles) is said to be haunted! Over the years, people have reported seeing the ghosts of knights, hearing voices, and witnessing other unexplained phenomena (amazing things that happen in nature or the world around us). "

Moosham Castle

Nobody knows who built Moosham Castle in Austria, but it is believed to have been constructed around 1191. However, this medieval castle is best known for its bloody and horrible history. Toward the end of the Middle Ages in Europe, witch trials increased. The most well-known and horrible trials occurred at Moosham Castle between 1675 and 1690. When we think of witch trials, we often think of women being accused, but most of the victims of these trials were young men and boys.

Aerial view of Moosham Castle.[24]

The Tower of London

We've already mentioned the famous Tower of London. However, this classic medieval castle is known for more than its architecture. Throughout its history, the Tower of London has served many purposes. It was a fortress, a royal palace, a prison, a place where executions were held, a military barracks, a records office, an observatory, and even a zoo!

During the Middle Ages in 1483, it was nicknamed the "Bloody Tower" following the disappearance and possibly murder of Edward V and the Duke of York. It was also famously where two of Henry VIII's wives, Anne Boleyn and Catherine Howard, were executed. Elizabeth I was a prisoner there before she was queen, as was Thomas Cromwell and other notable figures. As recently as 1941, the tower was used as a prison for one of Adolf Hitler's deputies, Rudolf Hess.

Château Gaillard

Richard the Lionheart, king of England, built the Château Gaillard castle to guard the Seine River Valley approach to Normandy in the twelfth century as a challenge to the French. At the time, Normandy was under his control. Richard I earned his nickname "Lionheart" thanks to his bravery in fighting during the crusades.

Château Gaillard.[25]

> **FUN FACT**
>
> Despite being king of England, Richard I only lived in England for less than a year. He spent most of his life abroad in France or fighting overseas battles.

Edinburgh Castle

Standing on Castle Rock in Edinburgh, Scotland, this castle is one of the oldest fortified places in Europe. Edinburgh Castle is one of the most important strongholds in Scotland and has withstood many sieges and seen many battles throughout its history. It's also one of the most attacked places in the world. During the Middle Ages between 1296 and 1346, Edinburgh Castle was a vital line of defense for the Scottish against the English in the *Anglo-Scottish Wars* or *Scottish Wars of Independence*.

A picture of Castle Rock in Edinburgh, taken from Princes Street Gardens below.[24]

Chapter 6 Activity

Write your own spooky story involving a castle and/or draw your spooky castle or monster/ghost!

Chapter 7: Incredible Medieval Faceoffs

Of course, all this medieval training to become a knight and building impressively strong castles had a purpose. If there's one thing that happened a lot during the Middle Ages, it was fighting. So, let's head into battle and travel back to some of the most incredible and memorable medieval faceoffs!

The Norman Conquest of England

Perhaps the most well-known conquest of the Middle Ages was in 1066. It's known as the *Norman Conquest of England*. England was inhabited and ruled by the *Anglo-Saxon* people from 410 until 1066. But on January 5, 1066, *King Edward the Confessor* died without any heirs.

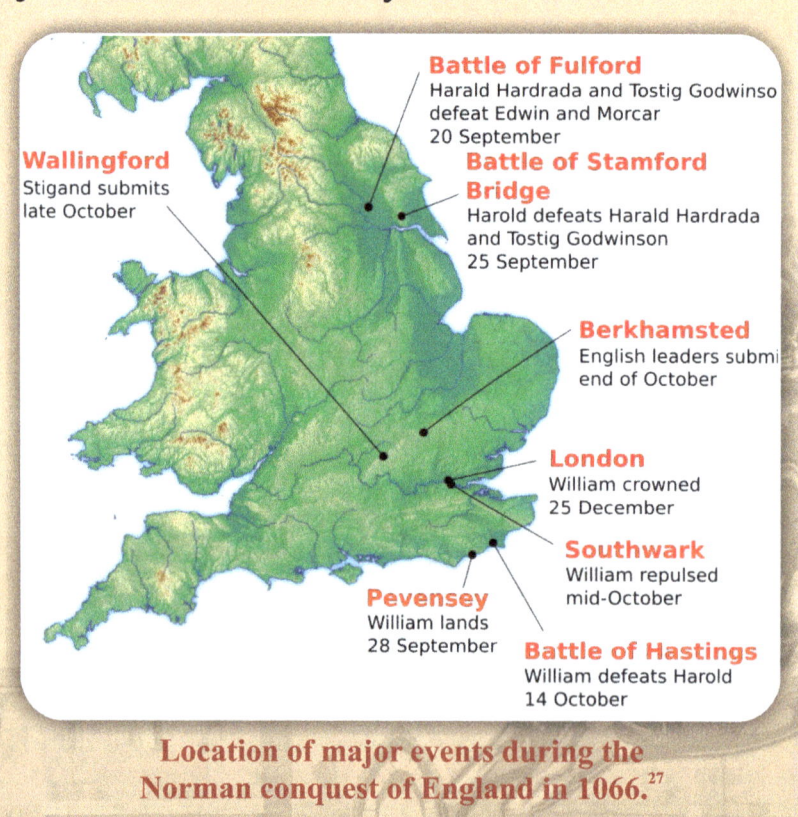

Location of major events during the Norman conquest of England in 1066.[27]

Two men claimed they should inherit the throne. *Harold Godwinson* was King Edward's brother-in-law. Harold was the Anglo-Saxon son of the powerful *Earl of Wessex* and related to *King Cnut the Great*, who once ruled over Norway, Denmark, and England. The day after King Edward died, he was named King Harold II.

However, another man who claimed the throne belonged to him was *William, Duke of Normandy*, later nicknamed William the Conqueror. He was also related to the late king through his uncle and said that King Edward had promised him the throne when he visited in 1051.

The Battle of Stamford Bridge

Others also tried to claim the throne. First, Harold had to squash an attempt by his brother *Tostig Godwinson*. Following a failed attempt to attack, Tostig was pushed into Scotland. The next time he invaded, he had the help of *King Harald III Hardrada of Norway*, who also felt he had a claim to the throne. On September 25, 1066, Harold II defeated and killed Tostig and King Harald Hardrada in the *Battle of Stamford Bridge* in Yorkshire.

However, William of Normandy and his forces finally arrived in southern England just three days after the battle. Tired from marching north and fighting, Harold's soldiers now had to march about two hundred miles south to meet William's army in Sussex!

The Battle of Hastings

The Battle of Hastings was a pivotal battle during the conquest. It started on October 14, 1066 when William's army was forced to advance on the Saxons. Both sides seemed equally matched and suffered high casualties. The Saxons had superior armor but fewer archers. Following a mistake in which Harold's army began to retreat, the Normans finally had their chance. They fired hundreds of arrows into the Saxon army. One hit ended the war. An arrow shot King Harold II in the eye, killing him. With no king or heir to fight for, the battle was over. William the Conqueror had won the throne of England!

The Saxons were unhappy about this and tried to put other people on the throne, but William continued to fight for the throne and eventually won. He was crowned king of England on December 25, 1066.

A section of the Bayeux Tapestry shows King Harold II's death during the Battle of Hastings.[28]

> ## Fun FACT
>
> "The famous Bayeux Tapestry is a piece of material that depicts the Norman conquest of England by William the Conqueror. It's on display in Bayeux, Normandy, France. It's nearly seventy meters long and fifty centimeters tall!"

The Hundred Years' War

During the Middle Ages, the longest war in history took place. Despite its name, it was actually longer than a hundred years—it lasted 116! The Hundred Years' War was a series of battles between England and France from 1337 until 1453. It was so long that five different kings ruled in both countries during this time.

So, what caused such a long war in the first place?

In 1328, the King of France died. The English king at the time, *King Edward III*, was also a duke of France. He believed he should become king of France, too. Ultimately, the French chose a French nobleman to rule, though: *Philip VI*. Edward III accepted this decision, and that should have been the end of it. However, Philip VI felt threatened by Edward III and decided to take control of the king's land in France. Understandably, Edward wasn't happy about this, so he decided to fight for control of France.

Of course, since it was such a long war, there were many significant battles with losses and wins for both sides.

The Black Prince

King Edward III's son, *Edward*, was nicknamed "the *Black Prince*." It is thought that he earned his name due to his distinctive black armor and shield. He was famed for his military skills and chivalric honor and was considered one of the greatest knights of the Middle Ages. He helped lead his father's army to many victories.

The Black Prince proved his worth during the *Battle of Crécy* in 1346. Despite being hugely outnumbered, the English won, with only about three hundred casualties compared to the French's fourteen thousand. The French called on their allies in Scotland for help. However, King David II of Scotland was captured and became Edward III's prisoner.

The Black Prince led his father's army during another important battle, the *Battle of Poitiers*, in 1356. The French army's leader was *King John II*, or *John the Good*. He was determined to prove his worth as a military leader and secure a French victory. Once again, the English were hugely outnumbered by the French army, with around seven thousand men against thirty-five thousand. But again, the English won, capturing King John II in the process.

A drawing of Edward the Black Prince.[29]

With the French king now England's prisoner, the war should have been over and treaties signed. Unfortunately, King John II died while in captivity, so war broke out all over again. The following battles were less successful for the English, and France won many. Starting in 1380, there was a period of peace. But in 1407, civil war broke out in France, and the English took the opportunity to strike again.

Joan of Arc

By 1428, England ruled most of France, and the French *King Charles VII* no longer had power. A sixteen-year-old peasant girl, *Joan of Arc*, claimed to have had a vision from God about a French victory.

A painting of Joan of Arc at King Charles VII's coronation.[30]

She convinced the king that God had chosen her to lead his army to victory—an incredible feat during a time when women did not fight in armies! Seventeen-year-old Joan led the army in the *Siege of Orléans* dressed in white armor with short hair. She helped the French win and helped the king get his crown back. She was even a guest at his coronation.

Sadly, Joan was later captured in battle and held prisoner. She was accused of being a witch and committing the crime of dressing in men's clothing. Despite Joan helping him to victory, King Charles VII didn't want to risk his crown by trying to rescue her. So, in 1431, at only nineteen years old, Joan was sentenced to death and burned at the stake.

> **Fun Fact**
> Joan of Arc became a Catholic saint in 1920 and is a patron saint of France.

By 1453, Joan's prediction had come true, and France finally defeated England, ending the war for good.

The Crusades

We've already mentioned the crusades, but now let's learn a little more about the battles during them. Lots of countries were involved in the crusades. Historians generally recognize nine official crusades, though there were many more unofficial crusades, too.

The First Crusade

The First Crusade started in 1095 when *King Alexius I* of the *Byzantine (biz-un-tyne) Empire* asked the Catholic Pope for help defending his land against the *Seljuk (sell-jook) Turks*.

Because the Holy Land of Jerusalem was in the Byzantine Empire, the pope encouraged people to fight against the Turks. He said that those who died in the war would be forgiven of their sins and go straight to heaven.

By 1099, the First Crusade had been successful, and new Christian states were established. When one of these was captured in 1144 by the Turks, a Second Crusade was launched. This time, the Christians failed. When the Muslims captured Jerusalem in 1187, the Third Crusade began. Although the Christians lost, a treaty was signed that said Christian pilgrims could still visit Jerusalem.

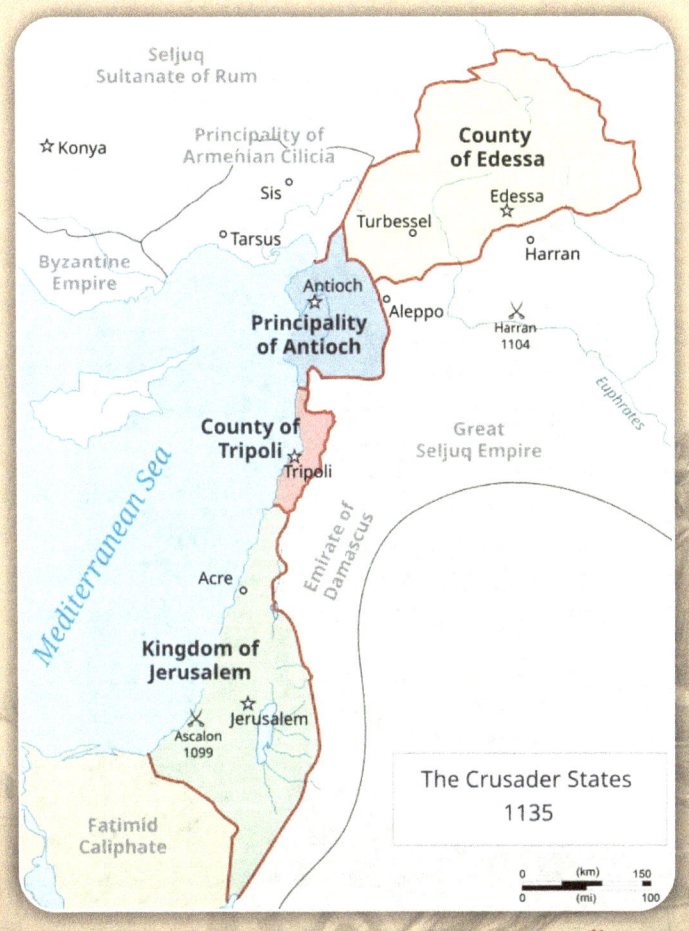

A map of the Crusader states in 1135.[31]

The Fourth Crusade of 1202 went terribly wrong as the Christians turned against each other. The people of Venice convinced the Crusaders to capture the competing Christian cities of Zara (in modern-day Croatia) and *Constantinople (con-stan-tin-oh-pul)* (in modern-day Turkey). After this, there was another Crusade in France in 1209 called the *Albigensian Crusade*.

The Children's Crusade

Next was the *Children's Crusade* of 1212. In France and Germany, children began forming bands, planning to march into the Holy Land and lead their own crusade.

The Children's Crusade.[32]

Why? A boy claimed Jesus had visited him in a vision and said he should go to peacefully convert Muslims to Christianity. The two groups of children made it to Italy, where they were put on boats to Morocco. But they never made it to the Holy Land. Many died during the difficult journey. It is believed that others who made it were sold into slavery.

Last Crusades

There were several more crusades after this. The Fifth Crusade of 1218 was reasonably successful, making it to Egypt. The Muslims offered to give up Jerusalem. However, the leader of the Fifth Crusade refused. This proved to be a silly choice since he was later defeated. The Sixth Crusade of 1228 had some success, too, gaining control of most of Jerusalem. But by 1244, the Turks took it back.

King Louis IX of France led the Seventh Crusade in 1249 and was captured and released a year later. This didn't stop him from trying again, though. He led the Eighth Crusade in 1270. This time it failed because he died from the plague.

The Ninth Crusade was led by the future king of England, *Edward I*, in 1271, but he soon signed a truce ending it. More small crusades were led over the next year. But in 1291, the Crusades officially ended when one of the final remaining Crusader states was defeated by Muslims.

Chapter 7 Activity

Circle the correct answer to the following questions.

1. Which people ruled England before the Norman Conquest?
    a. The Anglo-Saxons
    b. The Vikings
    c. The Celts

2. In which battle did King Harold II (Harold Godwinson) defeat his brother, Tostig Godwinson, and King Harald III Hardrada of Norway?
    a. The Battle of Hastings
    b. The Battle of Stamford Bridge
    c. The Battle of York

3. In what year was the Battle of Hastings fought?
    a. 1218
    b. 1095
    c. 1066

4. Who won the Battle of Hastings?
    a. William, Duke of Normandy (William the Conqueror)
    b. King Harold II (Harold Godwinson)
    c. King Harald III Hardrada of Norway

5. How many years did the Hundred Years' War last?
    a. 100
    b. 116
    c. 112

6. Which countries fought in the Hundred Years' War?

   a. England and Scotland

   b. France and Germany

   c. England and France

7. Who helped King Charles VII of France win the war for France following a vision from God?

   a. The Black Prince

   b. John the Good

   c. Joan of Arc

8. How many official crusades were there?

   a. 8

   b. 9

   c. 10

Chapter 7 Answers

1. Which people ruled England before the Norman Conquest?

    a. The Anglo-Saxons

2. In which battle did King Harold II (Harold Godwinson) defeat his brother, Tostig Godwinson, and King Harald III Hardrada of Norway?

    b. The Battle of Stamford Bridge

3. In what year was the Battle of Hastings fought?

    c. 1066

4. Who won the Battle of Hastings?

    a. William, Duke of Normandy (William the Conqueror)

5. How many years did the Hundred Years' War last?

    c. 116

6. Which countries fought in the Hundred Years' War?

    c. England and France

7. Who helped King Charles VII of France win the war for France following a vision from God?

    a. Joan of Arc

8. How many official crusades were there?

    b. 9

Chapter 8: Weapons and Armor: A Knight's Arsenal

So, now you know all about what it means to be a medieval knight and how to become one. You know about the castles you might be sworn to protect and the siege warfare and battles involved in protecting them. Now, let's discover the most important weapons and armor you need to keep you safe as a knight during the Middle Ages!

Armor

There were two main types of armor during the Middle Ages, chain mail and plate armor.

Chain mail

Chain mail was made from thousands of small interlinked rings of metal. Imagine a strong metal necklace chain connecting to other chains above and below—enough to cover your whole body—and that should give you an idea of what it looks like!

Fun Fact

> Early forms of chainmail worn in Roman times (thought to have originated in Asia) were made by sewing iron rings to fabric or leather clothing.

By the Middle Ages, chain mail was made by tightly welding interlacing rings together. Early designs were sleeveless. You would attach a chain mail sleeve for your sword arm. Later designs, worn during the Battle of Hastings, were long, with two full sleeves. You might also have a chain mail hood covering your face and neck under your helmet. Of course, as you can imagine, this armor was heavy and uncomfortable! Padded clothing was worn underneath to prevent bruises. By the twelfth century, soldiers' legs, feet, and hands were also protected by chain mail.

> **Fun Fact**
>
> " The main body of chain mail covering the torso and later the arms was called a hauberk (haw-berk). This could weigh up to thirty pounds! "

Despite being heavy, chain mail was flexible and moved with your body, making it easier to fight in. While it offered a decent amount of protection, it was vulnerable to arrows and thin swords. Because of this, some knights began putting plate metal over their more vulnerable places, such as their chests, to protect their

A reconstruction of a Norwegian medieval soldier's armor.[33]

hearts. Eventually, plate armor replaced chain mail as people covered their whole bodies with it instead.

Plate armor

Although plate armor offered better protection than chain mail, the knights had to sacrifice flexibility. And (believe it or not) plate armor was even heavier than chain mail. A full set weighed around sixty pounds! Still, by the 1400s, most knights wore this style of armor. Plate armor was made from several pieces of metal, each with a name. Separating the armor into smaller pieces made it easier to move in.

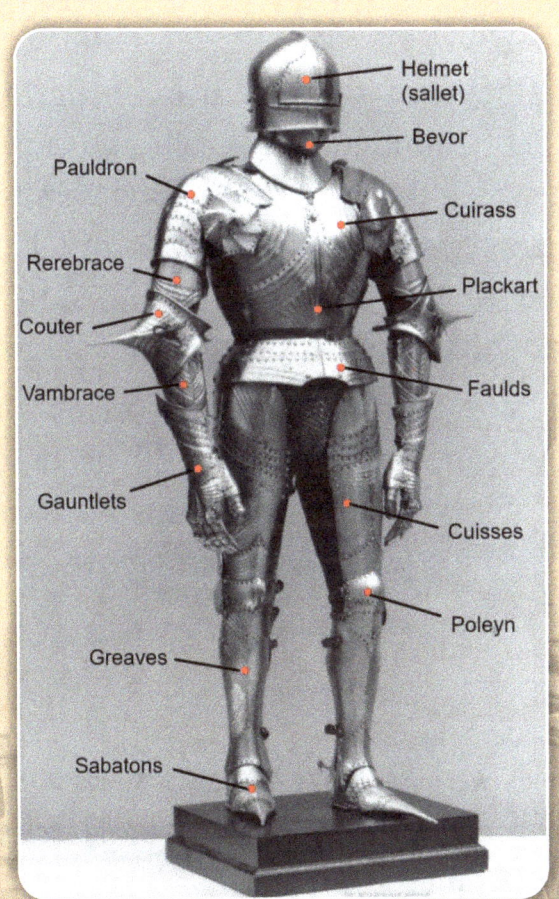

Late medieval Gothic plate armor with a list of elements. The slot in the helmet is called an ocularium.[34]

Shields

Medieval shields came in all shapes and sizes and could be small and light or big and heavy. They were made from strong wood and then covered in leather, and the rims were reinforced with metal. Here are some of the more common shapes of shields:

Round – Circular in shape, this was one of the oldest styles.

Kite – Rounded at the top and tapering down to a thinner rounded end, this style was used for riding on horseback.

Buckler – This was a small round metal shield that could be attached to the waist and held in one hand.

Heater – Developed in the twelfth century from the kite shield, it was less rounded at the top and not as narrow at the bottom. It was lighter than previous versions and cheap to make, making it popular with people of all classes. It was often decorated with a coat of arms or family crest. This is perhaps the most iconic shield for medieval knights.

Pavise – This large rectangular and convex shield was big enough to cover the entire body and used for protection against arrow attacks. It was developed around the end of the fourteenth century. It, too, was painted with a coat of arms.

> **FUN FACT**
>
> " Pavise shields were so heavy that there was a special job for someone to carry them! People would hold them in place to protect others. "

A photo of different types of shields at a modern-day medieval fair.[35]

Weapons

Now that you're fully protected by your armor of choice, what weapon will you wield as a knight? You've got lots to choose from! In addition to the weapons below, soldiers of the Middle Ages would use daggers, axes, spears, and more.

Sword

Perhaps the most important medieval weapon was the sword. This weapon was used to stab or slice your opponent and caused a great amount of damage with little effort. Sword fighting was a medieval skill, almost an art form. It helped people believe that even against a bigger, stronger opponent, you could still win if you were more skillful.

Because they were expensive, swords were more common for knights to own than common soldiers. Swords were also a status symbol. Because it was possible to wear your sword and carry it off the battlefield, it showed others that you were wealthy enough to afford and use one.

There were many styles of swords. Some were small, light, and easier to wield with one hand, while others were big, long, and required two hands to lift. Blades could be curved or straight, vary in thickness, and have one or two sharp edges. Swords needed to be strong enough not to break when used. The type of sword you'd want would also depend on the armor your enemy was wearing.

Lance

We've already mentioned lances and how they were used during jousts. These may have been used for popular entertainment, but they were also used in battle. The only way to wield your lance was on horseback. The tip of your wooden lance would have a metal spike. With the force of your horse charging toward your enemy, it could cause serious damage or even death. If nothing else, a lance was a way to knock enemy soldiers off their horses. However, you only got one chance to use your lance, and it was not good for close combat.

A drawing of a knight in armor riding on horseback carrying a lance.[36]

Longbows and arrows

This type of bow and arrow became popular in the Middle Ages since it allowed the user to attack his enemy from a distance and fire over the walls of a castle. It became a crucial part of medieval warfare. Longbows earned their nickname because they were almost as tall as, if not taller than, the user—around six feet! The best longbows were made of yew wood and required a lot of strength to fire. As much as 180 pounds of force would be needed to fire them! Longbows could travel anywhere between 450 and 1,000 feet depending on the arrow used. This was a vitally important weapon during the Hundred Years' War.

Fun Fact

" Some knights thought it was cowardly to use a longbow, as you did not need to fight your opponent in close combat. "

Crossbow

Crossbows were an ingenious weapon that was powerful enough to penetrate armor. The main body was made from wood, the bow from steel, and the bowstring from horn. Crossbows required a lot of skill to make, but they were highly effective. They were incredibly easy to use and more powerful compared to longbows. Soldiers needed little training to take down armored soldiers with them. They were especially useful in siege warfare.

Fun Fact

" The crossbow was so effective that, in England, only knights could use it. This was perhaps because it was seen to be unfair and unchivalrous to use such a deadly weapon in high numbers. "

Fifteenth or sixteenth-century crossbow from central Europe.[37]

Mace

A mace is a type of club with a heavy head at the end that could also be spiked to deliver blows to your opponent. It was popular in the Middle Ages because it was easy to use and good for close combat. The head of a mace could be made from practically anything as long as it was strong and heavy!

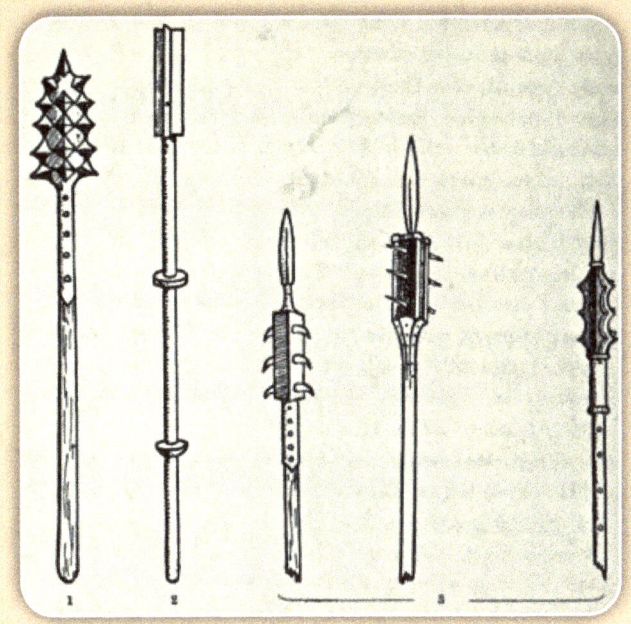

This picture shows different types of blunt weapons used in medieval times. On the far left are the morning star and the mace. The following three are all maces.[38]

Warhorse

A horse might not sound like a weapon, but a well-trained warhorse could save your life! Your horse needed to be brave and not shy away from blood and fighting. It wouldn't be easily scared and would follow your command. A knight's warhorse was called a *destrier (des-tree-er)*. Warhorses wore armor, too! It would cover more vulnerable areas such as its head, neck, and sides.

Fun Fact

" War horses were a medieval knight's prized possession—and likely most expensive! Owning a good war horse was a bit like owning a sports car today. "

Chapter 8 Activity

Create and draw your ideal knight's armor and weapons! Be sure to label what you've chosen. Remember that you only have two hands, so you can't have them all!

Or

Make your own medieval shield and sword from cardboard and other household items by following the video tutorials below!

Shield: https://youtu.be/NmTJUjSG_PY?si=D4S_5InYfNAYVnqb

Sword: https://youtu.be/sjnIhp_TBPc?si=anboZZGtgx-8Q4M7

If you want to learn more about tons of other exciting historical periods, check out our other books!

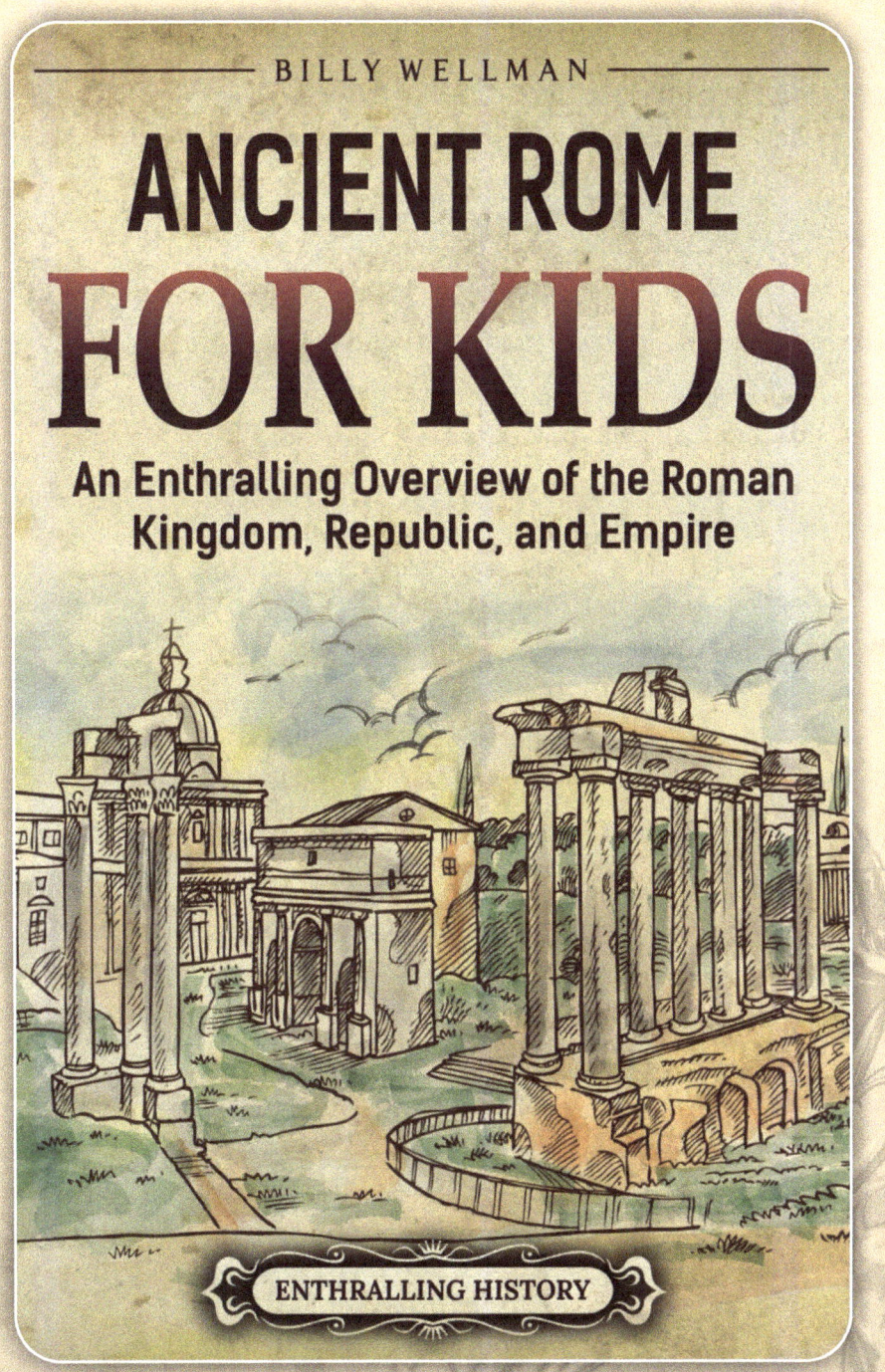

Further Reading

Books

Dixon, Philip. Knights and Castles. Simon & Schuster. 2007.

Gravett, Christopher. Eyewitness: Castle. DK Publishing. 2000.

MacDonald, Fiona. You Wouldn't Want to Be a Medieval Knight! Scholastic. 2013.

Educational Websites

BBC Bitesize: History – The Middle Ages https://www.bbc.co.uk/bitesize

The British Museum – www.britishmuseum.org

National Geographic Kids: Knights and Castles https://kids.nationalgeographic.com

Historic UK – www.historic-uk.com

English Heritage: Kids' History https://www.english-heritage.org.uk

YouTube Resources

"How to Build a Medieval Castle" – Simple History https://www.youtube.com/@SimpleHistory

"Life in a Medieval Castle" – Smithsonian Channel https://www.youtube.com/@SmithsonianChannel

Castle Model DIY Tutorial https://youtu.be/HGH2bteGpTA

Image Sources

[1] By Lordoftheloch - Own work, CC0, https://commons.wikimedia.org/w/index.php?curid=24714870

[2] [Duncan] from Nottingham, UK, CC BY 2.0 <https://creativecommons.org/licenses/by/2.0>, via Wikimedia Commons, https://commons.wikimedia.org/w/index.php?curid=32007084

[3] https://commons.wikimedia.org/w/index.php?curid=2855833

[4] https://commons.wikimedia.org/w/index.php?curid=480730

[5] https://commons.wikimedia.org/w/index.php?curid=1197015

[6] https://commons.wikimedia.org/w/index.php?curid=24276510

[7] https://commons.wikimedia.org/w/index.php?curid=36370988

[8] https://commons.wikimedia.org/w/index.php?curid=1844091

[9] Colin Babb, CC BY-SA 2.0, https://commons.wikimedia.org/w/index.php?curid=13238627

[10] Null, CC0, via Wikimedia Commons, https://commons.wikimedia.org/w/index.php?curid=29123142

[11] https://commons.wikimedia.org/w/index.php?curid=14909937

[12] https://commons.wikimedia.org/w/index.php?curid=106183978

[13] https://commons.wikimedia.org/w/index.php?curid=308092

[14] diego_cue, CC BY-SA 3.0 <https://creativecommons.org/licenses/by-sa/3.0>, via Wikimedia Commons, https://commons.wikimedia.org/w/index.php?curid=53901372

[15] Clarinetlover, CC BY-SA 3.0 <https://creativecommons.org/licenses/by-sa/3.0>, via Wikimedia Commons, https://commons.wikimedia.org/w/index.php?curid=18525281

[16] https://commons.wikimedia.org/w/index.php?curid=1299630

[17] Internet Archive Book Images, No restrictions, via Wikimedia Commons, https://commons.wikimedia.org/w/index.php?curid=43536090

[18] https://commons.wikimedia.org/w/index.php?curid=37055303

[19] https://commons.wikimedia.org/w/index.php?curid=7868719

[20] https://commons.wikimedia.org/w/index.php?curid=74745989

[21] https://commons.wikimedia.org/w/index.php?curid=46336984

[22] www.bdmundo.com, CC BY-SA 2.0 <https://creativecommons.org/licenses/by-sa/2.0>, via Wikimedia Commons, https://commons.wikimedia.org/w/index.php?curid=57204361

[23] John Baker, CC BY-SA 2.0 <https://creativecommons.org/licenses/by-sa/2.0>, via Wikimedia Commons, https://commons.wikimedia.org/w/index.php?curid=144736122

[24] Arne Müseler / www.arne-mueseler.com, CC BY-SA 3.0 DE <https://creativecommons.org/licenses/by-sa/3.0/de/deed.en>, via Wikimedia Commons, https://commons.wikimedia.org/w/index.php?curid=98353440

[25] Sylvain Verlaine, CC BY-SA 3.0 <https://creativecommons.org/licenses/by-sa/3.0>, via Wikimedia Commons, https://commons.wikimedia.org/w/index.php?curid=28520758

[26] Scglossop1, CC BY-SA 4.0 <https://creativecommons.org/licenses/by-sa/4.0>, via Wikimedia Commons, https://commons.wikimedia.org/w/index.php?curid=110110095

[27] Amitchell125 at English Wikipedia, CC BY 3.0 <https://creativecommons.org/licenses/by/3.0>, via Wikimedia Commons, https://commons.wikimedia.org/w/index.php?curid=34995896

[28] https://commons.wikimedia.org/w/index.php?curid=25609093

[29] https://www.onthisday.com/people/edward-the-black-prince, CC BY-SA 4.0 <https://creativecommons.org/licenses/by-sa/4.0>, via Wikimedia Commons, https://commons.wikimedia.org/w/index.php?curid=129519011

[30] https://commons.wikimedia.org/w/index.php?curid=3876400

[31] Amitchell125, CC BY-SA 4.0 <https://creativecommons.org/licenses/by-sa/4.0>, via Wikimedia Commons, https://commons.wikimedia.org/w/index.php?curid=103890901

[32] Terry, Arthur Guy, Sheila Thibodeau Lambrinos Collection - York University, No restrictions, via Wikimedia Commons, https://commons.wikimedia.org/w/index.php?curid=43154661

[33] By Wolfmann, CC BY-SA 4.0 <https://creativecommons.org/licenses/by-

sa/4.0>, via Wikimedia Commons, https://commons.wikimedia.org/w/index.php?curid=110930063

[34] https://metmuseum.org/art/collection/search/21928, CC0, via Wikimedia Commons, https://commons.wikimedia.org/w/index.php?curid=129759858

[35] Kobretti, CC BY-SA 3.0 <https://creativecommons.org/licenses/by-sa/3.0>, via Wikimedia Commons, https://commons.wikimedia.org/w/index.php?curid=16317421

[36] https://commons.wikimedia.org/w/index.php?curid=88542466

[37] By Metropolitan Museum of Art, CC0, via Wikimedia Commons, https://commons.wikimedia.org/w/index.php?curid=65052196

[38] https://commons.wikimedia.org/w/index.php?curid=95141370